To

From

For Ben   A.H.

Text by Christina Goodings
Illustrations copyright © 2011 Annabel Hudson
This edition copyright © 2011 Lion Hudson

The moral rights of the author and illustrator
have been asserted

A Lion Children's Book
an imprint of
Lion Hudson plc
Wilkinson House, Jordan Hill Road,
Oxford OX2 8DR, England
www.lionhudson.com
ISBN 978 0 7459 6206 1

First edition 2011
1 3 5 7 9 10 8 6 4 2 0

Acknowledgments
The Lord's Prayer (on page 221) from *Common
Worship: Services and Prayers for the Church of England*
(Church House Publishing, 2000) is copyright ©
The English Language Liturgical Consultation,
1988 and is reproduced by permission of the
publishers.
The prayer on page 222 is adapted from the
Good News Bible published by the Bible Societies
and HarperCollins Publishers, © American Bible
Society 1994, used with permission.

A catalogue record for this book is available
from the British Library

Typeset in 16/20 Baskerville MT Schoolbook
Printed in China July 2011 (manufacturer LH06)

Distributed by:
UK: Marston Book Services Ltd, PO Box 269,
Abingdon, Oxon OX14 4YN
USA: Trafalgar Square Publishing, 814 N Franklin
Street, Chicago, IL 60610
USA Christian Market: Kregel Publications,
PO Box 2607, Grand Rapids, MI 49501

My Look and Point Bible

Christina Goodings
Illustrated by Annabel Hudson

LION
CHILDREN'S

contents

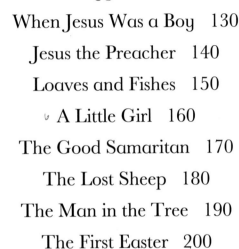

Old Testament

In the Beginning

In the beginning was a dark and stormy nothing. Perhaps it was a bit like a billowing black cloud that the wind tugs and tumbles.

whooo

Perhaps it was a bit like a dark and stormy sea where the water swells and dips.

crash

Into that nothing, God spoke:
"Let there be light."

glitter

shine

sparkle

God was beginning to make the world.
God made the sky.

sun

moon

stars

God made the sea.

waves

fish

whale

shells

seahorse

crab

God made the land and everything in it.

tree

sheep

butterfly

hill

flower

lion

rhino

elephant

snail

frog

12

God made people to live in the world and take care of it.
"Everything I have made is for you to enjoy," said God.
"But stay away from one tree. Its fruit will harm you."

bird

Adam

Eve

rabbit

lizard

13

One day, Eve was by the fruit tree.

"Are you wondering?" asked a sneaky voice.

"Because I'm wondering too. I'm wondering why God said the fruit would harm you.

"I think it looks very good."

It was a snake speaking.

fruit

Eve

snake

"I shall try some," said Eve.

15

Adam and Eve knew at once they had disobeyed.
  "Oh dear," said God. "That's really spoiled things."

hornet

thistle

thorn

hungry
grub

dig

dig dig

"We're on our own now," said Adam. "We'll have to make the best of it."

"We'll find a way," said Eve. But she looked sad.

"I wish we could be friends with God again," she sighed.

Noah and the Flood

G od made a good world.
But it got mixed up with bad things

One man was good. His name was Noah.
  He kept flocks of animals.

Noah

sheep

goat

God spoke to Noah.
  "I am going to wash away the old world," said God.
  "Listen to what you must do."
  Noah listened. Then he and his three sons set to work.

Noah and his boys built a great big boat.
   Noah's wife helped with the plan too, and
so did his sons' wives.
   They helped load food onto the boat.

beans

onions

apples

hay

pumpkin

The next part of the plan was to fetch all the animals:
a mother and a father of every kind.

zebras

parrots

sheep

elephants

rhinos

bears

rabbits

doves

lions

peacocks

mice

goats

23

Then came the rain.

pitter
patter

It flooded the whole wide world.

coo

For days and days and weeks and weeks the ark
floated on the water until...

BUMP!

squawk

aargh

miaow

"We've hit land!" cried Noah.

Not long after, Noah sent a dove to fly further than he could see. It brought back something in its beak.

green leaf

bear

snore

"Not too long to wait," said Noah.

yawn

It still seemed like a long time.

At last the flood was over. Noah and his family
and all the animals came out of the ark.
  "Begin my world again," said God.
  "Look at colours in the sky, and remember this.

rainbow

"I promise that the world will have summer and winter
and seedtime and harvest for ever."

Abraham and His Family

Long ago lived a man named Abraham. He could trace his family all the way back from his father to his father's father and so on to Noah.

But there was a problem. Abraham wasn't a father.

"God has blessed me with many good things," he sighed.

cradle

But no baby.

"What's the use of all the things I have?" he sighed.

sheep

servants

donkeys

cows

goats

camels

His wife, Sarah, was sad too.

Especially when she sat watching one of the servants and her young son.

blanket

toddler

toy

pet lamb

"I think I'm too old to have a baby now," Sarah said
to herself.
    That night, she fell asleep feeling as sad as ever.

Abraham sat outside longer.

He remembered what God had said to him long before.

"You will have children. Your family will be as many as the stars in the sky. They will be my family. They will show the whole world how they can be my family."

Abraham tried to count the stars.

star

He couldn't count them all.

star

moon

star

star

faraway
star

Then one day, Sarah told him amazing news.
  "I'm expecting a baby!" she laughed.
  Abraham began to see new things around the place.

blanket

toys

baby clothes

But he didn't mind a bit.
  Especially when he saw his son.

Isaac

"Everything I have will one day belong to him," he said.
"Don't let the camels get too close," said Sarah anxiously.

Baby Isaac grew up.

toddler

boy

teen

man

Abraham was delighted to find just the right girl for
him to marry.

"May God bless you," he said to the happy couple.
"May you have children, and may they have children."
In his heart he knew that God's own family was growing.

flowers

Isaac

wedding

Rebekah

Joseph and the Dream Come True

J oseph was feeling proud.
"My great grandfather was Abraham, my grandfather
was Isaac, and my father is Jacob," he said.

sheaf

"And I'm the most important of all Jacob's sons.
"That's why he gave me this expensive coat.
"That's why I have special dreams. In my dream,
I made a sheaf that stood up tall and all my brothers'
sheaves bowed down to it."

Joseph's big brothers were jealous. One day they made a wicked plan.

"Look: there are some traders going to market in Egypt. We can sell our boastful brother as a slave."

no coat

coins

trader

They ripped the coat and took a torn piece home.
  "This is all we have left of Joseph," they told their father.
  "He must have been eaten."
They told him of the wild animals they had seen.

jackal

lion

bear

Jacob wept.

In faraway Egypt, Joseph became a slave. He worked hard and was good at his job.

poor slave

rich man

mouse

cat

But someone told lies about him to get him into trouble. Joseph went to prison. But God had not forgotten him. In fact, God helped Joseph to explain dreams.

So when the king of Egypt had a puzzling dream, someone sent for Joseph.

"I dreamed of seven fat cows," said the king. "Then seven thin cows came and ate them.

fat cow

thin cow

"I dreamed of seven fat ears of corn. Then seven thin ears came and ate them.

thin corn

fat corn

"I can explain," said Joseph. "There will be seven good harvests and then seven bad harvests.

"We must store the extra food from the good harvests to feed us in the bad ones."

"Thank you," said the king. "Storing will be your job."

Joseph became a very important man.
He made sure people stored lots of grain in barns.

barn

grain
sack

chariot

servant

Then came the bad harvests.
  In the land where Jacob lived with his family,
there was nothing to eat.

little
brother

no grain

"We hear there is grain in Egypt," said the ten
thin brothers. "We shall go and buy some."

The brothers arrived and bowed down to the man
in charge of the grain.
"Let us buy some food," they begged.

"Please."

"For our
father Jacob."

"And our little
brother Benjamin."

They didn't know that they were bowing to Joseph.
His old dream had come true.

Jacob

Joseph

At last, Joseph understood.

"God has kept me safe so I can keep all of us safe now," he said.

"Come and make your home in Egypt."

So all of Jacob's family came and stayed.

Benjamin

watermelon

Moses and the Great Escape

Joseph and his brothers had families. There were children and grandchildren – and the family became a nation: the children of Israel.

The new king of Egypt was angry and scared.

"Make them work. I need bricks for my palaces," he said.

straw

water

brick

mud

king

"There are still too many of them," said the king to his soldiers.

"Go and find all the baby boys. Throw them into the river."

tramp tramp 49

One mother made a plan.

"We shall hide your baby brother by the river," she said to her daughter, Miriam. "We shall make a basket into a floating cradle."

baby

toy

lid

blanket

basket

They put the floating cradle in the reeds.
  Miriam watched.

bzz

flit

quack

51

The princess came to bathe. She waded down to the river. She asked her maid to bring her the thing she could see in the reeds. Together they lifted the lid.

"It's a baby!

princess

maid

"I shall take care of him," said the princess. "I shall call him 'Moses'. But I'll need someone to help me."

Miriam ran forward.

"I shall find someone," she said. "Someone good with babies."

She brought her mother.

"I will pay you to look after him," said the princess.

"I love him already," said Miriam's mother.

tickle
tickle

When Moses grew up, he was angry to see how the king treated his slaves.

But being angry led to a fight.

After the fight, Moses had to run and hide.

In the faraway desert, he saw something amazing.

fire

bush

leaf

He heard God speaking.

"Go and set the slaves free," said God.

Moses went and asked the king of Egypt.
The king said no.

No no no

"There will be trouble," said Moses. And there was.

frogs

There was all kinds of trouble… and still more.

locusts

flies

55

At last the king changed his mind.

"Go now!"

Moses led all the children of Israel out of Egypt.

God made a path for them where usually there was sea.

fish

They went back to the land where Joseph had been born: the land where God wanted the people to make their home.

Moses

Miriam

tambourine

Joshua and the New Home

Moses led the people of Israel out of Egypt. They travelled for a long time through a dry and dusty land.

God looked after them so they had food to eat and water to drink.

manna

quail

mountain

tent

water

59

One day, on a mountain top, God told Moses the laws the people must obey: laws to help them do what is good and right.

The laws were carved into stone.

Moses

"Love God."

tablets of stone

"Love one another."

But Moses was growing old. He chose a brave young man named Joshua to be the next leader.

"Teach the people to obey the laws," Moses told Joshua.

Joshua

Spear

"Then God will be our God. We will be God's people. God will keep us safe and the land will be our home."

Joshua led the people into that land: Canaan.
  Other people already lived there.
  "God will help us make it our home," said Joshua.
"Here's what to do with the first city."

Jericho city

For six days they marched
around the city.

march march march

On the seventh…
   The walls fell down. Joshua and his soldiers took the city.

CRASH

trumpet

priest

soldier

Joshua and the people believed that God helped them
settle in the land.

   It was a good place. The people could grow good
harvests.

There was pasture for their animals.

fields

sheep

pet lamb

65

Joshua made his own home in the land. When he was growing old, he asked all the people to come and visit him.

Joshua's home

"Think of the all the things God has done to help us," he said.

"Long ago, I promised to obey God's laws. All my family agree to obey God's laws. Will you obey God's laws?"

"Yes we will!"

"Always!"

"Me too."

Naomi and Ruth

The land of the people of Israel was a good place to be. Naomi lived in the town of Bethlehem with her husband and two sons. Together they grew good crops.

Naomi

barley

mouse

68

Then one year, the harvest failed.

Naomi and her family set off for another land: the land of Moab.

There, each of the sons got married.

kiss

kiss

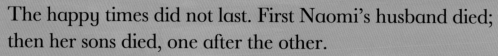

The happy times did not last. First Naomi's husband died; then her sons died, one after the other.

Naomi made a plan. "We shall go back to my home in Bethlehem," she told the two wives.

So they set out.

They had not gone far when Naomi stopped.

"Oh dear," she said. "I'm not being fair to you two.

"You should go back to your mothers. Maybe you will have a chance to marry again."

One agreed to go.

Goodbye

Ruth

"I'll stay with you."

sandals

stick

The other, Ruth, begged Naomi
to let her travel on.
"I will worship your God,"
she said.

71

When the two reached Bethlehem, people came out to welcome Naomi.

"Tell us your news," they said.

"I only have sad news," said Naomi. "I have no family except Ruth.

"I don't even have grandchildren." She burst into tears.

"There there."

sob

cat

Then they walked on past waving fields of barley.
  It was harvest time.

mouse

barley

Ruth had an idea.
  "I shall go and pick up the leftover stalks of barley.
That way, we'll have food."

So Ruth went to the fields in the early morning.
  The farmer, Boaz felt sorry for her.
  "Take care of her," he told his servants. "She is being
so kind to poor old Naomi."
  And they did.

sheaf

mouse

But that wasn't all. The more Boaz saw Ruth, the more he liked her.

Naomi found out about that, and she really wanted Boaz and Ruth to marry.

BOaz

Ruth

water jar

bread

At last it was all agreed.
  Boaz arranged to marry Ruth.
  Naomi felt happier than ever.

There was a big party for the wedding.

jingle jangle

dancing feet

Not long after, Ruth and Boaz had a son.
"God has taken care of all of us," she said.

rock-a-bye

awah

77

Samuel

In the land of the people of Israel was a place of worship: a place to pray to God and give thanks. All the people tried to go there once a year, bringing gifts.

fathers

mothers

children

gifts

A woman named Hannah went there with her husband. She cried as she said her prayer.

"I hope you're not drunk," said Eli, the priest.

Place of worship

Hannah

Eli

"I'm just sad," sobbed Hannah, "because I have no children.

"I am praying for a baby. If ever I have a son, I will bring him here to be your helper."

79

The very next year, Hannah and her husband had a baby.

sleeping

They loved watching little Samuel grow.

crawling

walking

running

When he was old enough, Hannah took him to Eli.

"God answered my prayer," she told him. "Please let my Samuel be your helper."

"I will take care of him," said the priest.

"And I'll be back to visit him," promised Hannah.

Eli gave Samuel an important job: to keep the lamps burning in the place of worship.

1 2 3 4 5 6 7

lampstand

Just to be sure, Samuel even slept in the place of worship.
  One night, he heard a voice calling him.
  "Samuel, Samuel."
  "I'm coming, Eli," he said.

sleeping
mat

He went to Eli's room.

Here I am

Eli was surprised. "I didn't call you," he said. "Go back to bed."

But Samuel heard the voice a second time, and then a third.

At last Eli understood. "God is calling your name," he said. "Next time, tell God you are listening."

So Samuel did.

God spoke to Samuel in the place of worship.

God told him that he would grow up to be the leader of his people.

And Samuel grew up trusting in God.

As a man, he became a great leader.
   "Remember this," he told the people.
   "Worship God, and God alone.
   "Then God will bless us and take care of us."
   The people listened to Samuel, and lived in peace.

When Samuel was old he chose a king to rule the people.
Saul was brave and strong.

Old Samuel

crown   King Saul

Brave David

When David was little, he loved to hear the story of his great-grandmother.

"Her name was Ruth," his mother told him. "She came to Bethlehem from far away. She trusted the God of our people, and God blessed her."

mother

David

wool

David learned to say prayers to God.

Then, because he liked singing, he made his prayers into songs.

He made a harp and played along.

tra la

harp

pling pling

David became the shepherd boy of the family.

He looked after the sheep. He trusted God to look after him.

So he sang this song.

"God is my shepherd, tra la.
God cares for me, alleluia!
He leads me where the grass is green
And where the pools are clear and clean."

baa baa baa

He also got good at using his slingshot.
With it he threw stones that HIT.
That scared the wild animals.

stone...

ping

sling

lion

At that time, the king of Israel was Saul. Three of David's brothers were among his soldiers.

One day, David was sent to take them a food parcel.

As they ate, they told him about the enemy.

"Look: there's Goliath."

"If just one person beats him, the enemy army will give in."

munch
munch

sack

"He's taller and stronger than everyone else."
"And he has the best weapons."

javelins

helmet

armour

spear

shieldbearer

sword

"I'll fight him," said David.
 "You're too little," said his brothers.

NO   NO   NO

Saul

"I can beat wild animals," said David to the king. "I can beat Goliath."

In the end, they let him go. No one else dared.
   David walked to the stream.
   He chose five pebbles.

stick

bag

sling

5

pebbles

1 2 3 4

David went and shouted to Goliath.
 "You don't scare me. I trust in God."
 Then, to everyone's amazement…

whee

David had won. He went on to beat all the enemies
of his people.

He became king after Saul.

Always, he was brave.

Always, he trusted God.

plunk

thud

Jonah Learns a Lesson

Jonah was in a hurry.
He knew for sure that God had told him to go to Nineveh.

God had said, "Tell the people of Nineveh to stop being bad and start being good…

"Or something dreadful will happen to them."

But Jonah was hurrying away from Nineveh.

"Wait for me!"

sea

shore

98

sailor

boat

99

Jonah got on a boat that was sailing far away.
   Then a storm blew up.

whoooo

crash

"It's my fault," said Jonah. "I'm running
away from God.
   "Help me overboard, please."
   The sailors didn't want to
be unkind.

Jonah sank down, down, down.

bubble bubble

fish

fish

big fishy
something

The big fishy something swallowed Jonah

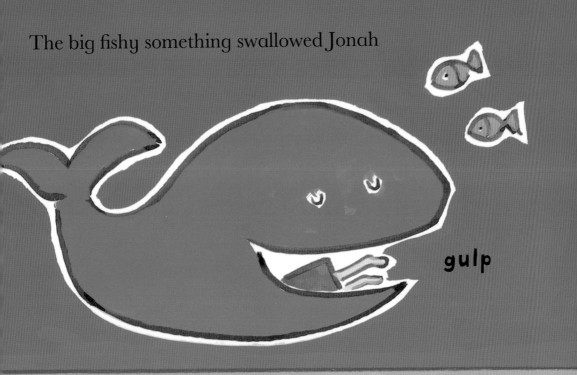

gulp

and took him to a beach.

oof

103

"I understand, God," said Jonah.
  "You want me to go to Nineveh."
  So he went.

plod plod plod

He told the people to stop being bad and start being good.
They listened and were sorry.

And God forgave them.

Jonah was angry. "I wanted them punished," he sulked.
He went off and sat in a little shelter

sun

"It's hot," he said.

So God made a plant grow
and give him shade.

worm

plant

wilt...

"Poor plant. You were my friend!" Jonah wailed.

"You care about a plant, do you?" said God.

"Well, I cared about the people of Nineveh, and the children, and the animals."

HOORAY

Daniel and the Lions

Daniel was good and Daniel was wise.
For that reason, the Great King of Persia and
Most of the Rest of the World gave him an important job.

king

Daniel

Some people were jealous.

They went to the king.

"O Great King: make it a law to worship you and you alone," they said.

"Good idea," replied the king.

grovel bow smirk

The law was made. The men went to spy on Daniel.

He was saying prayers to his god: the God of the people of Israel.

window

Look

They took Daniel to the king.

"We found Daniel saying prayers to his God," they said.

"That means he doesn't worship you alone."

The king knew Daniel was his loyal servant.
But he had made the law.
And he had agreed a punishment.

112

soldiers

march march

He told his soldiers to take Daniel to the lions.

Daniel was thrown into the den.
God sent an angel to keep Daniel safe.
"Come all you gentle lions
And listen to my song
Don't eat up poor old Daniel
For he has done no wrong."

singing angel

lioness

rrah

grrr

yawn

zzzzz

Meanwhile, the king was fretting.
The next day he rushed to the den
of lions.
   "Are you alright, Daniel?" he called.
   "I'm well," said Daniel.
"God has taken care of me."

snore

snore

The king had Daniel lifted from the pit.

"Listen, everyone," he said. "Daniel's God is the greatest god."

"Now, where are the liars who got Daniel in this mess?"

"After them!"

run   run   run

New Testament

Baby Jesus

Mary lived in the town of Nazareth. She was looking forward to getting married.

Mary

needle

thread

dress

miaow

120

One day, an angel came to visit.

"Don't be afraid," said the angel. "God has chosen you to have a baby.

"He will be God's Son. You will name him 'Jesus'."

"I will," agreed Mary.

Mary's husband-to-be was Joseph. He was sad.

"I can't marry her now," he said. "She's having someone else's baby."

tools

carpenter's tool

wood

workbench

saw

eek

But in a dream, an angel spoke to him.

"The child is God's. Please look after him... and Mary too."

Joseph agreed to take care of Mary.

pack

donkey

lizard

stony road

At that time, the emperor who ruled the land and many others wanted everyone counted.

Joseph went to his home town of Bethlehem.

"We will be counted as husband and wife-to-be," he told Mary.

innkeeper

Lots of people had to go to Bethlehem, just like Mary and Joseph.

When the two got there, all the rooms for visitors were taken.

"No room," said the innkeeper.

Then someone remembered about the stable.
"We can make that cosy for the night," they said.
And there in the stable, Mary's baby was born.

Joseph

donkey

Mary

Baby Jesus

manger

ox

On the hillside nearby, shepherds were watching their sheep.

Angels appeared.

Alleluia

shepherds

angels

sheep

"A new king has been born," they sang.
"Go and find him."

star

pack

camel

gift

path

In a country far away, wise men saw a star.
  "A new king has been born," they agreed.
"We must find him."

127

When they arrived, they gave their gifts: rich gifts
for a baby king.

myrr[

frankincense

gold

129

When Jesus Was a Boy

Jesus grew up in Nazareth.
From Joseph he learned to be a carpenter.

Jesus

tools

Joseph

wood

He went to school with the other boys. Like them, he learned to read. He learned to read the stories of his people, which were written on scrolls.

schoolroom

teacher

scroll

The most important story was about Moses, and the first Passover.

Every year Mary and Jesus went to the Temple in Jerusalem for the Passover festival. When Jesus was twelve, he went too.

JOSEPH

Mary

JeSuS

Temple

priest

teachers

133

After the festival, everyone from Nazareth set off for home together.

donkey

heehaw

plod plod plod

At the end of the day, they began to set up camp.
"Where's Jesus?" asked Mary.
She asked first one person then another.
No one had seen him.

tent

camp fire

pot

twit twoo

moon

Mary and Joseph were frantic.
They rushed back to the city.

136

137

At long last Mary and Joseph found Jesus.
   He was in the Temple, talking to the teachers.

clever
boy

"Where have you been?" scolded Mary.
"I was so worried."
   "In my Father's house," said Jesus.

Even so, it was time to go back home. Jesus went and was a good son.

workshop

grown-up Jesus

wooden toy

happy child

Jesus the Preacher

Jesus had a cousin named John.

John

rough cloak

wild hair

John was a preacher. Many people came to listen to him. He told them it was right to obey God: to be honest and fair.

Lots of people agreed to stop doing bad things and make a new beginning. John baptized them in the river.

splish

One day Jesus came to John.

"Please baptize me," he said.

"You haven't done bad things," replied John.

But he understood: Jesus wanted to mark a new beginning.

As John lifted Jesus out of the water, he saw a dove land on Jesus' head. God's voice said, "This is my Son."

dove

Jesus went into the wild country to think.
   Did he want to be rich, famous, and powerful?
   "No," said Jesus. "I know what God wants. All you bad thoughts: goodbye."

wild hills

wolf

lizard

stones

thorns

After that, Jesus became a preacher.

He began to tell people how to live as God's friends.

He told them about God's love.

He showed the power of God's love by healing those who were sick.

"Hooray!"

Jesus knew he needed help to spread the message.
He began to choose people to be his disciples. He began
with four fishermen.

Andrew

Peter

John

James

boat

nets

fish

145

Jesus often went by boat to the towns and villages around Lake Galilee.

One evening, after a busy day, Jesus got in the boat and fell asleep.

The disciples sailed the boat.

Then a storm blew up.

flapping sail

Help

wind

oar

147

The disciples woke Jesus.
  He stood up and spoke:
  "Wind: be still.
  "Waves: calm down."

sunrise

gull

calm water

At once the storm was still.

"Who is this Jesus?" the disciples asked.
"Even the wind and waves obey him."

Loaves and Fishes

In the towns and villages of Galilee, all the talk was of Jesus.

People wanted to listen to his teaching.

People wanted to see his miracles.

So one day, Jesus and his disciples went off for a rest.

But someone saw them, and the news spread.

The crowds came hurrying.

over there

run run run

tree

chirrup

shade

blanket

151

Jesus welcomed the people.
  All through the day he talked to the crowds.
  He healed those who were sick.
  As always, he welcomed children.
  The people stayed all day.

morning

noon

afternoon

sunset

yawn

The disciples began to worry. They went to Jesus.
  "It's time to stop," they said. "Send the people away
so they can get a meal. There's nothing out here."
  "You should take care of them," said Jesus.
"What food have you got?"

"Not a lot," said Andrew. "This young boy has some he's happy to share."

"Thank you," said Jesus. "Ask the people to sit down for a meal."

five loaves
two fish

When the people were ready, Jesus said the mealtime prayer.

His disciples took the food and handed pieces out.

People took some and passed it on.

By a miracle, there was enough for everyone.

"Here you are."

"Thank you."

"Now," said Jesus to his disciples. "We don't want any waste. Please gather up the scraps."

They did so, and they filled twelve baskets.

Meanwhile, the people began to talk.
 "Jesus is the best preacher ever."
 "Let's ask him to be king."
But Jesus wasn't going to be that kind of king.
He slipped away.

twit twoo

Jesus

A Little Girl

D own by the lake, crowds were waiting for Jesus to arrive.

boat

Hooray

lake

shore

A man named Jairus rushed up to Jesus.

"Please come to my house," he said. "My little girl is ill. Please make her well."

Jesus and Jairus began to walk along the street. But the crowds were jostling. Everyone wanted to be close to Jesus.

shove   push

It was slow going.
Jairus was in tears.

squawk

163

Then Jesus stopped.
  "Who touched my cloak?" he asked.

A woman stepped forward.

"It was me," she said. "I've been unwell for so long. I wanted to touch you and be better."

And at once she knew: she was healed.

Me

coo

A messenger came running.

"Jesus need not come," he said. His face was sad.

"Your little girl has died."

Jesus walked on to Jairus' house.
    Family friends were there, weeping.

He went into the house. Jairus and his wife took him to the little girl's room.

"Little girl, get up."

yawn

toy

bed

miaow

Jesus turned to the parents.

"Your little girl will be hungry," he said. "I think it's time to get a meal ready."

169

The Good Samaritan

A man came to Jesus with a question:
"What must I do to be friends with God for ever?"
"You know what our holy books say," replied Jesus.
"I do," said the man. He was a teacher. "You must love God and your neighbour.
"Who is my neighbour?" asked the man.
And Jesus told this story:

teacher

holy book

A man was going from Jerusalem to Jericho.
On the way, robbers came and beat him up.

It so happened a priest from the Temple was going that way.
He saw the man lying in the road.
He saw that he was hurt.
But the priest hurried by on the other side.

oh dear

road   priest

Next came another man. He was a helper in the Temple.
He came and had a look at the man.
"Oh dear, oh dear," he said.

Temple
helper

vulture

hmm

Then he hurried on by.

Next came a foreigner, a Samaritan.

He had nothing to do with the Temple. No one said he was important.

But he saw the man and felt sorry for him.

Samaritan

bandage

He cleaned the man's wounds. He wrapped them in bandages.

Then he helped the man onto his donkey.

donkey

hee haw

He took him to an inn.

blanket

grapes

jug

bed

The next day, the Samaritan went to the innkeeper.

"I have to travel on," he said. "But here is money. Look after the man who was hurt. If it costs more, I will pay next time."

innkeeper

penny

"Now what do you think?" Jesus asked the teacher. "Who was a good neighbour?"

"The one who was kind," came the answer.

"Then you go and do the same," said Jesus.

The Lost Sheep

Wherever Jesus went, lots of people came to see him. "He calls himself a teacher," said some. "But what kind of teacher mixes with that lot?"

Jesus told a story.

rich people

old people

unwell people

healthy people

poor people

young
people

good
people

disgraceful
people 181

There was once a shepherd who had a hundred sheep. He took them to fields of green grass. He led them to pools of clear water.

sheep

pool

grass

frog

reed

One day, when the shepherd was counting,
he found he only had 99.

98   97   96   95   94

oh dear

99

So he left the 99 safely grazing and off he went.

"Bye!"

"Take care!"

184

plod plod plod

stick

185

He searched behind rocks.

ssss

He looked among thorns.

tweet

He peered down holes.

wiffle

He peeked over scary edges.

caw

186

But many hours went by before he found the sheep.

Gently he picked up his sheep and carried it home.

"Let's have a party," he said, "for I have found my lost sheep."

tootle too

"God is like that shepherd," said Jesus. "God cares for the people who have strayed from the right path. And when they are found, the angels sing."

The Man in the Tree

I t was a fine day in spring, and the streets
of Jericho were crowded.

Jesus was coming and everyone wanted to see him.

woof

At the back of a crowd was a very short man. Zacchaeus couldn't see. But no one cared, because they didn't like him. He was a tax collector, and he cheated them out of money.

Zacchaeus had an idea.

But then Jesus came. He stopped by the tree.
  "Come down, Zacchaeus," he called. "I want to come to your house today."

Why him?

Zacchaeus hurried down and led Jesus to his house.
  He offered the very best.
  Jesus told Zacchaeus the things he told everyone:
about how to be friends with God.

pomegranates

grapes

jug of drink

"Change your ways," he said.
"I will," replied Zacchaeus.

Today

Zacchaeus stood up.

"I'm going to give half of all I have to the poor," he declared.

"I'm going to repay the people I've cheated.

"I'm going to make a new start."

Jesus was very pleased.

And so were all the people of Jericho.

The First Easter

It was time for a festival. Everyone who could was going to Jerusalem, to the Temple there.
Jesus and his disciples were among them.

Hosanna

When the crowd saw Jesus, they were excited.
"Look!" they said. "Perhaps Jesus is coming to be our king. That would be good." And they began to cheer.

God save the king

wave

palm branch

Jesus went to the Temple.

The festival market was in full swing.

"This is wrong," said Jesus. "The Temple should be a place to say prayers."

He began to chase out the people who were buying and selling – and cheating one another.

203

After that, Jesus and his disciples got ready for the festival. In an upstairs room, they laid the feast.

Jesus broke the bread and sighed. "My body will soon be broken," he said.

He passed round the cup of wine. "My blood soon will be spilt," he said.

The disciples wondered what he meant.

cup of wine

But one was thinking about other things: Judas had been talking to the people who didn't like Jesus. He had a wicked plan.

And soon he slipped away...

out the door

broken bread

Soon after, Jesus and his disciples went to an olive grove to sleep.

As Jesus was saying his prayers, Judas came with soldiers to put him on trial.

There

Everything was a bad as it could be. The people who didn't like Jesus had him put to death on a cross alongside two criminals.

That evening, just before sunset, some of Jesus' friends laid the body in a tomb.

Jesus' friends spent the next day as sad as they could be.
The day after, just before sunrise, some women went to
the tomb.

The door was open.

They saw angels.

"Jesus is not here!"

"He is risen!"

empty tomb

They could hardly believe the news.
"Can it be true?"

Ever After

Jesus

Jesus was alive. He came and spoke to his friends.

"Remember," he said, "all I told you about God's love.
"What has happened to me is a sign: God's love is stronger than everything.

"I want you to tell that to all the world."

After that, Jesus went to God in heaven.

But Jesus' friends and disciples didn't feel very brave.
How would they dare tell people about Jesus?
They stayed indoors, hiding, until one day…

… everything changed. They felt that God had come among them. They believed God had given them strength.

dancing
flame

7   8   9   10   11   Matthias

213

They rushed out into the streets of Jerusalem. The disciple named Peter stood up.

He told the crowds about Jesus. He told them how to live as God's friends.
  And many people believed.

As the news about Jesus spread, all kinds of people believed.

I do

I do

I do

Those who believed were baptized.

Even people who had been enemies of Jesus began
to believe.
   Soon Jesus' followers began taking the news
to many different lands.

Paul

boat

In time, the news spread all over the world.
Just as the children used to gather round Jesus to hear what he had to say, so children gather today.

The Prayer Jesus Taught

Our Father in heaven,
hallowed be your name,
your kingdom come,
your will be done,
on earth as in heaven.
Give us today our daily bread.
Forgive us our sins
as we forgive those who sin against us.
Lead us not into temptation
but deliver us from evil.

For the kingdom, the power,
and the glory are yours
now and for ever.

Amen.

A Shepherd Boy's Psalm

Dear God, you are my shepherd,
You give me all I need,
You take me where the grass grows green
And I can safely feed.

You take me where the water
Is quiet and cool and clear;
And there I rest and know I'm safe
For you are always near.

Based on Psalm 23